T0114819

GRADES **K-3**

Phonemic Awareness

The **READING PUZZLE**

Elaine K. McEwan
Michelle Judware
Darlene Carino
Candace Darling

CORWIN PRESS
Classroom

For information:

Corwin Press
A SAGE Company
2455 Teller Road
Thousand Oaks, California 91320
CorwinPress.com

SAGE, Ltd.
1 Oliver's Yard
55 City Road
London EC1Y 1SP
United Kingdom

SAGE India Pvt. Ltd.
B 1/I 1 Mohan Cooperative
Industrial Area
Mathura Road, New Delhi
India 110 044

SAGE Asia-Pacific Pvt. Ltd.
33 Pekin Street #02-01
Far East Square
Singapore 048763

ISBN: 978-1-4129-5820-2

This book is printed on acid-free paper.

08 09 10 11 12 10 9 8 7 6 5 4 3 2 1

Executive Editor: Kathleen Hex
Managing Developmental Editor: Christine Hood
Editorial Assistant: Anne O'Dell
Developmental Writers: Michelle Judware, Darlene Carino, Candace Darling
Developmental Editor: Carolea Williams
Proofreader: Carrie Reiling
Art Director: Anthony D. Paular
Design Project Manager: Jeffrey Stith
Cover Designers: Michael Dubowe and Jeffrey Stith
Illustrator: Ben Mahan
Design Consultant: The Development Source

GRADES **K–3**

Phonemic Awareness

The READING PUZZLE

TABLE OF CONTENTS

Introduction

Students who have developed phonemic awareness are aware that spoken words are made up of a series of sounds called *phonemes.* Phonemic awareness is one of the best indicators that students will successfully develop the necessary reading skills over time. And, it is an essential prerequisite to mastering the sound-spelling correspondences in phonics.

The primary objective of this resource is to provide support in the development of phonemic awareness through oral language activities. Students will be invited to chant, play games, sort pictures, and sing. Through these engaging activities, students will learn to hear the sounds that make up words and then begin to play with those sounds by blending, segmenting, and manipulating them.

The phonemic awareness skills in this resource are presented in a logical and systematic way. They are divided into five categories:

- Recognizing rhymes
- Identifying sounds
- Blending sounds
- Segmenting sounds
- Manipulating sounds

The activities address a variety of learning styles. Kinesthetic learners will be able to jump and move. Auditory learners will enjoy listening to the sounds of language. Visual learners will use picture clues to stimulate their minds and memories. Each student will have the opportunity to be successful in the journey toward phonemic awareness.

When possible, present a new activity in a small-group setting. This will enable you to target the skills required to meet each student's specific needs. After providing initial instruction, use the activities with a whole group or at independent learning centers. The activities require very little preparatory work so you can spend more time planning for and providing differentiated instruction.

These activities have been designed to help you provide engaging lesson content, capture students' interests, meet individual needs, and encourage skill practice. Building phonological awareness will pave the way for student achievement and a lifelong love of reading.

978-1-4129-5820-2

Put It Into Practice

What do you think of when you hear the word *code*? Maybe you picture a secret code you developed as a child, text messaging codes, or maybe Morse code. Whatever the case, a code is a systematic arrangement of symbols that represent meaning. The most important code to students who do not know how to read is the English alphabet code. In order to learn to read, students must acquire an intimate knowledge of the code—the conventionally accepted way in which letters or groups of letters correspond to spoken sounds in the English language.

Three pieces of the Reading Puzzle are needed to help students access code knowledge: phonological awareness, phonics, and spelling. Each of these pieces is essential, for without phonological awareness skills to distinguish words, syllables, and individual sounds, students will struggle in phonics instruction. Many students need phonics instruction to learn how to decode (blend sounds together to read the words printed on the page) and encode (translate spoken and thought words into correctly spelled words).

The Reading Puzzle is a way of organizing and understanding reading instruction, as introduced in my book, *Teach Them All to Read: Catching the Kids Who Fall Through the Cracks* (2002). The puzzle contains the essential reading skills that students need to master in order to become literate at every grade level. *The Reading Puzzle, Grades K–3* series focuses on five of these skills: Vocabulary, Comprehension, Fluency, Phonics, and Phonemic Awareness.

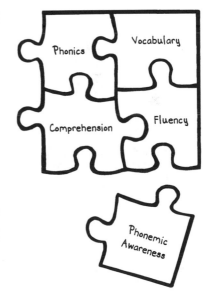

What Is Phonemic Awareness?

Phonemic awareness is the ability to identify and manipulate the sounds of letters and words, including: blending sounds to make words, creating rhyming patterns, and counting phonemes (individual sounds). It is the foundation upon which all other reading skills are built. Without phonemic awareness, students will be unable to identify the sounds in the word *sat*. Students must be able to identify the sounds of the word *sat* in order to change the word to *mat*. They then build on their skills to identify the letter that changed the word.

The Importance of Phonemic Awareness

Before students can identify letters, spell, comprehend, or read fluently, they must be able to hear and manipulate the individual phonemes in words. This skill is a critical prerequisite to acquiring the English language code needed to read. Numerous studies have demonstrated a link between phonemic awareness and success in early reading.

Students who cannot hear the individual phonemes in spoken words are unable to take the next step in acquiring the ability to read—learning how these sounds correspond to letters of the alphabet.

Effective early education teachers have instinctively known the importance of listening activities, word play, and rhyming games. Students need these language skills to be successful at learning to read. Early instruction and intense, directed remediation will help to increase the opportunity for reading success in all students.

How to Teach Phonemic Awareness

Phonemic awareness is best taught before formal reading instruction begins. Ideally, begin in early kindergarten or first grade at the latest. For older students with reading difficulties, begin awareness skills immediately. Phonemic awareness instruction is most effective when the following are present:

- Sufficient direct instruction and coaching before students work independently (I do it)

- Ample opportunities for practice after teacher modeling (We do it)

- Many opportunities for independent student practice (You do it)

- Frequent review and reinforcement of material taught previously

- Systematic, explicit, and supportive instruction

- A program with defined scope and sequence from words to syllables to phonemes

- The gradual addition of phonics

- Attention to segmenting, blending, and detection

- Instructors who accurately pronounce individual sounds

A successful phonemic awareness program should be thoughtfully planned. It is essential to assess students, find excellent professional development resources, and continually reinforce your training. If you adopt a published program, choose one that focuses on helping students notice phonemes in words and make connections between phonemes in words and letters of the alphabet. Make sure that the sequence of activities moves from words to syllables to sounds. Then, follow-up with letters of the alphabet. Anticipate that some students may not respond to whole-group instruction. Provide opportunities for small-group and individual instruction.

Phonemic awareness is a vital piece of the Reading Puzzle. Helping students build these skills will provide a solid foundation on which to build their future reading success!

978-1-4129-5820-2

CHAPTER 1

The Road to Rhyme

The recognition of rhyme is the starting point for the development of phonemic awareness. Using rhyming-word activities in early learning encourages students to play with language and identify sounds that are alike. The ability to generate a list of rhyming words is an important step in developing phonemic awareness.

Rhyme Around

1. Refer to the lists on the **Rhyming Word Families reproducibles (pages 8–10)**. Write the "Rhyme Around" song on chart paper. Teach the song to students and invite them to sing along.

    ### Rhyme Around
    (Tune: "London Bridge")
    Rhyming words are all around, all around, all around.
    *Rhyming words are all around—***fish**, **wish**, **dish***.*

2. Have students sing the song several times before challenging them to replace the words *fish, wish,* and *dish* with new rhyming words. Provide students with the first new word and invite them to think of two more words that rhyme with the new word.

    Rhyming words are all around, all around, all around.
    *Rhyming words are all around—***hat**, ____, ____*.*

    In this example, students may suggest the words *cat* and *mat* to complete the rhyming word trio.

3. Continue this activity using other rhyming word families, including those with blends, digraphs, and long-vowel spellings.

Rhyming Word Families

-ab	-ack	-ad	-ail
cab crab	back snack	dad sad	fail snail
grab jab	pack quack	had add	mail rail
tab gab	rack crack	mad fad	nail sail
lab blab	sack black	pad glad	pail tail

-ain	-ake	-ale	-all
gain train	bake brake	bale whale	call ball
main stain	cake take	pale tale	fall stall
pain brain	make wake	sale scale	hall tall
rain chain	rake flake	male stale	mall wall

-am	-ame	-an	-ank
ham slam	came flame	ban plan	bank thank
jam spam	game same	can tan	tank crank
ram lamb	fame tame	fan man	rank blank
yam gram	name shame	ran pan	sank drank

-ap	-ar	-ash	-at
cap scrap	car tar	cash trash	bat chat
gap nap	bar scar	bash dash	cat sat
map tap	far star	hash crash	hat pat
lap flap	jar guitar	rash smash	mat rat

-ate	-ay	-eal	-ear
date state	day tray	deal veal	dear clear
hate fate	hay ray	heal real	fear near
late crate	pay bay	meal steal	gear rear
mate plate	play gray	seal squeal	hear tear

Rhyming Word Families

-eat		-ed		-eel		-eep	
beat	seat	red	fled	heel	steel	beep	sheep
heat	wheat	bed	shed	peel	wheel	deep	sleep
meat	treat	fed	sled	feel		jeep	sweep
neat	cleat	led	shred	reel		keep	weep

-ell		-en		-ent		-est	
bell	well	den	ten	bent	sent	best	rest
sell	spell	hen	then	cent	went	jest	test
yell	shell	men	when	dent	scent	nest	vest
tell	smell	pen	wren	lent	spent	pest	west

-ice		-ick		-id		-ide	
dice	slice	kick	stick	hid	did	hide	wide
nice	price	lick	thick	lid	kid	ride	slide
mice	twice	pick	quick	rid	grid	side	bride
rice	spice	sick	trick	slid	squid	tide	glide

-ight		-ile		-ill		-in	
fight	sight	vile	tile	hill	chill	pin	thin
light	tight	pile	smile	mill	grill	win	grin
might	right	mile	while	pill	spill	shin	skin
night	bright	file	reptile	still	drill	spin	chin

-ind		-ine		-ing		-ink	
bind	wind	mine	line	king	spring	link	wink
find	hind	pine	fine	ring	sting	pink	think
kind	blind	nine	dine	sing	bring	rink	blink
mind	grind	vine	spine	wing	swing	sink	shrink

Rhyming Word Families

-ip		-ish		-it		-oat	
tip	skip	fish	squish	bit	kit	goat	moat
lip	ship	dish	radish	fit	pit	coat	throat
hip	slip	wish	polish	grit	sit	boat	bloat
grip	trip	swish	finish	hit	quit	float	gloat

-ock		-og		-oil		-oke	
dock	flock	dog	log	oil	toil	woke	spoke
lock	frock	fog	frog	boil	coil	joke	stroke
rock	clock	hog	smog	foil	spoil	poke	broke
sock	block	jog	clog	soil	broil	smoke	choke

-ook		-oom		-op		-ore	
book	look	boom	vroom	mop	flop	tore	chore
cook	nook	room	broom	pop	stop	sore	score
hook	shook	zoom	bloom	crop	shop	wore	snore
took	brook	loom	gloom	drop	chop	more	store

-ot		-ow		-ow		-own	
dot	spot	blow	show	cow	vow	down	clown
not	blot	crow	slow	bow	wow	gown	crown
pot	trot	flow	snow	how	brow	town	brown
cot	plot	grow	throw	now	plow		

-uck		-ug		-ump		-unk	
duck	suck	bug	drug	bump	pump	bunk	trunk
luck	truck	jug	plug	dump	stump	junk	flunk
buck	stuck	mug	snug	jump	plump	hunk	skunk
tuck	cluck	rug	shrug	lump	thump	sunk	chunk

Reproducible

A Rhyme a Day

Set aside a few minutes at the beginning of each day to practice oral language. When students are beginning their journey to phonemic awareness, challenge them with a rhyme a day. Write several sentences on the board or chart paper. Underline a word in the sentence and leave the last word blank. See the sample sentences for ideas. Read the sentence aloud and invite students to complete it using a word that rhymes with the underlined word. As students master the skill, allow them to create their own sentences.

Sample Sentences

I saw a <u>cat</u> sit on the ____.

A broken <u>car</u> cannot go very ____.

The <u>boy</u> got a new ____.

One <u>day</u> I had nothing to ____.

The <u>goat</u> was in a ____.

I had to <u>dig</u> to find my ____.

Can an <u>elf</u> sit on a ____?

My <u>dad</u> was very ____.

Did the <u>dog</u> sit on the ____?

She is <u>not</u> on a ____.

The <u>cook</u> could not find her ____.

I <u>fell</u> on the ____.

Have You Ever?

Students love hearing about people or animals in humorous situations. Say a sentence about an animal and invite students to finish the sentence with a word that rhymes with the animal name. Introduce a visual learning component by holding up a picture card or toy animal when saying the animal name.

Sample Sentences

Have you ever seen a . . .

<u>giraffe</u> learning to ____? *(laugh)*

<u>shark</u> sitting in the ____? *(park)*

<u>seal</u> sitting on a ____? *(wheel)*

<u>cat</u> sleeping in a ____? *(hat)*

<u>cow</u> saying ____? *(meow)*

<u>pig</u> wearing a ____? *(wig)*

<u>bear</u> rocking in a ____? *(chair)*

<u>rat</u> wearing a ____? *(hat)*

<u>goat</u> rowing a ____? *(boat)*

<u>hen</u> counting to ____? *(ten)*

<u>mouse</u> building a ____? *(house)*

<u>sheep</u> driving a ____? *(jeep)*

<u>frog</u> jumping over a ____? *(hog)*

<u>deer</u> shouting a ____? *(cheer)*

<u>fly</u> wearing a ____? *(tie)*

<u>bug</u> giving a ____? *(hug)*

Classroom Creatures

Read the story, *There's a Wocket in My Pocket* by Dr. Seuss. Discuss the rhymes throughout the story. Encourage students to think about how the words rhyme, although one word is not a real object. To get the creative juices flowing, ask students to visualize each object as you read aloud the imaginary word.

Tell students they are going to make up their own silly, imaginary words. Prior to the activity, write the sentences on sentence strips and place them in a pocket chart. Model how to complete the activity by reading the sentence. Then insert an imaginary word: *There's a* <u>plunch</u> *in my* <u>lunch</u>.

Once students understand what to do, invite them to insert their own imaginary words into the sentences. As students develop mastery of the skill, ask them to create sentences for one another.

Sample Sentences

There's a _____ in my <u>lunch</u>.

There's a _____ in my <u>backpack</u>.

There's a _____ on the <u>easel</u>.

There's a _____ on the <u>globe</u>.

There's a _____ on the <u>flag</u>.

There's a _____ in my <u>folder</u>.

There's a _____ on my <u>friend</u>.

There's a _____ in the <u>sink</u>.

There's a _____ on my <u>teacher</u>.

There's a _____ on the <u>computer</u>.

There's a _____ on the <u>board</u>.

There's a _____ on the <u>sticker</u>.

There's a _____ on my <u>crayon</u>.

There's a _____ in my <u>glue</u>.

There's a _____ on the <u>shelf</u>.

There's a _____ on the <u>rug</u>.

There's a _____ on the <u>floor</u>.

There's a _____ on the <u>chalk</u>.

There's a _____ on the <u>map</u>.

There's a _____ on my <u>paper</u>.

There's a _____ on my <u>desk</u>.

There's a _____ on my <u>pencil</u>.

There's a _____ on my <u>book</u>.

There's a _____ on my <u>chair</u>.

978-1-4129-5820-2

Rhyme Time

Do a variety of the following physical activities in which students identify words that rhyme. Use words from the Rhyming Word Families reproducibles (pages 8–10).

Excer-Squatters

1. Explain to students that rhyming words sound the same at the end. As an example, explain that the words *bat* and *fat* rhyme because they both end with /ăt/. Remind students that not all words rhyme. The words *cat* and *man* do not rhyme because *cat* ends in /ăt/ and *man* ends in /ăn/.

2. Invite students to stand with their feet apart and their hands on their hips. Tell them that you are going to say a pair of words. If the words rhyme, students will squat down and then stand back up. If the words do not rhyme, students will remain standing. This is a great activity to see who understands the concept and who needs additional practice. It's great exercise too!

3. Model the first few rhyming pairs and have students watch what you do. Explain why you squat or remain standing. Invite students to join you in standing and squatting as you recite word pairs.

Sample Rhyming Word Pairs

cat–rat (squat)	get–tell (stand)	fish–rock (stand)
run–red (stand)	miss–meet (stand)	look–cook (squat)
bug–hug (squat)	sand–hand (squat)	wig–big (squat)
fan–can (squat)	fun–sun (squat)	clock–block (squat)
wood–car (stand)	pig–jig (squat)	can–tar (stand)

Walk It Out

Invite students to walk in a circle as you say a list of words. For each word that follows the rhyming pattern, have students take one step. When they hear a word that does not rhyme, have students sit down. For example, say: *red, bed, fed, led, fled*. As you say each word, students will take a step, walking in a circle. Then say: *stick*. When students hear the word *stick*, they should sit down since that word does not rhyme with the others.

Jumping Beans

Have students sit in a circle. Say a word from the Rhyming Word Families reproducibles (pages 8–10). Invite students to think of words that rhyme. Repeat this chant to students: *Can you rhyme it? Give a try. If you can, jump up high.* If students can think of a rhyming word, invite them to jump up and say their word.

Rhyming Rosie Says

Play a game similar to Simon Says that challenges students to recognize rhyming words. Give students a command, such as *touch your toes, raise your right hand,* or *hop on one foot*. Then say a word from the Rhyming Word Families reproducibles (pages 8–10). Before students follow the command, ask one student to say a word that rhymes with your word. If the student can provide a rhyming word, all students perform the command. If the word does not rhyme, they do not follow the command.

978-1-4129-5820-2

Puzzle Rhymes

Since this fun activity is self-correcting, it can be used in a variety of ways. Give each student their own set of pieces for individual practice. Copy the completed cards on cardstock and laminate them for a game in the literacy center. Or, create a musical chairs game using the puzzle pieces, so students can interact and move around the room.

1. Give each student a copy of one or more pages of the **Puzzle Rhymes reproducibles (pages 16–19)**. Point out to students that there is a picture on one side of the puzzle but not on the other. Invite them to think of a word that rhymes with the picture and draw it on the connecting half of the puzzle.

2. When students have finished drawing their rhyming words, invite them to carefully cut apart their puzzle pieces. Students can store their puzzle pieces in an envelope or resealable plastic bag.

3. Invite students to match their puzzle pieces with a partner or independently at a literacy center. Each puzzle piece has a unique connecting line so that only pictures of words that rhyme will fit together. This makes the activity self-correcting when students are working independently.

ABC Rhyme with Me

1. Reproduce the **ABC Rhyme with Me reproducibles (pages 20–28)**. Cut apart the poem cards. Explain to students that you are going to read aloud a rhyming poem for each letter of the alphabet. As you read the first poem, pause before saying the last word. Ask students to think of a rhyming word that would finish the sentence.

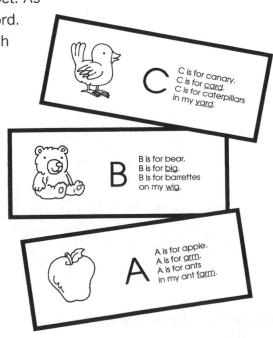

C is for canary.
C is for card.
C is for caterpillars
in my yard.

B is for bear.
B is for big.
B is for barrettes
on my wig.

A is for apple.
A is for arm.
A is for ants
in my ant farm.

2. Select a student to provide a rhyming word. If the student suggests a word that rhymes, give him or her the letter poem. Continue through the alphabet, giving the poems to students as they supply rhyming words.

3. Use the blank poem strip on page 28 to create additional poems using blends or digraphs. For example, *SH is for shower. SH is for sheep. SH is for Shana trying to sleep.*

Puzzle Rhymes

Directions: Draw a picture of something that rhymes with the object shown. Color and cut out the puzzle pieces.

Name _____ Date _____

Puzzle Rhymes

Directions: Draw a picture of something that rhymes with the object shown. Color and cut out the puzzle pieces.

Puzzle Rhymes

Directions: Draw a picture of something that rhymes with the object shown. Color and cut out the puzzle pieces.

Name _____ Date _____

Puzzle Rhymes

Directions: Draw a picture of something that rhymes with the object shown. Color and cut out the puzzle pieces.

ABC Rhyme with Me

A

A is for apple.
A is for <u>arm</u>.
A is for ants
in my ant <u>farm</u>.

B

B is for bear.
B is for <u>big</u>.
B is for barrettes
on my <u>wig</u>.

C

C is for canary.
C is for <u>card</u>.
C is for caterpillars
in my <u>yard</u>.

Reproducible 978-1-4129-5820-2 • © Corwin Press

A B C Rhyme with Me

D is for dragon.
D is for <u>dog</u>.
D is for ducks
dancing on a <u>log</u>.

E is for elephant.
E is for <u>end</u>.
E is for eleven letters
I need to <u>send</u>.

F is for feather.
F is for <u>fun</u>.
F is for friends
frolicking in the <u>sun</u>.

ABC Rhyme with Me

G is for gopher.
G is for <u>goat</u>.
G is for girls
riding in a <u>boat</u>.

H is for hamburger.
H is for <u>hot</u>.
H is for horses
on the <u>trot</u>.

I is for igloo.
I is for <u>inch</u>.
I is for insects that
might bite and <u>pinch</u>.

Reproducible   978-1-4129-5820-2 • © Corwin Press

ABC Rhyme with Me

J

J is for jar.
J is for <u>jeep</u>.
J is for jellybeans
that I will <u>keep</u>.

K

K is for koala.
K is for <u>kittens</u>.
K is for kings who
wear warm <u>mittens</u>.

L

L is for lemon.
L is for <u>lip</u>.
L is for lions
who love to <u>skip</u>.

ABC Rhyme with Me

M

M is for monkeys.
M is for <u>mice</u>.
M is for me
rolling the <u>dice</u>.

N

N is for nest.
N is for <u>not</u>.
N is for noodles
boiling in a <u>pot</u>.

O

O is for ostrich.
O is for <u>ox</u>.
O is for the octopus
who wears <u>socks</u>.

ABC Rhyme with Me

P

P is for panda.
P is for <u>peel</u>.
P is for pigs
who like to <u>squeal</u>.

Q

Q is for quilt.
Q is for <u>queen</u>.
Q is for quacking
ducks on the <u>green</u>.

R

R is for radio.
R is for <u>red</u>.
R is for Rita
resting on her <u>bed</u>.

ABC Rhyme with Me

S

S is for spider.
S is for <u>socks</u>.
S is for snakes
sliding out of a <u>box</u>.

T

T is for turtle.
T is for <u>toes</u>.
T is for tigers
licking my <u>nose</u>.

U

U is for unicorn.
U is for <u>under</u>.
U is for umbrellas in
the rain and <u>thunder</u>.

V

V is for vase.
V is for <u>vest</u>.
V is for violins
playing their <u>best</u>.

W

W is for watch.
W is for <u>wish</u>.
W is for whales
swimming with <u>fish</u>.

X

X is for <u>extra</u>.
X is for <u>X ray</u>.
X is for exiting
when you can't <u>stay</u>.

Y

Y is for yarn.
Y is for <u>year</u>.
Y is for yachts
docking at the <u>pier</u>.

Z

Z is for zip.
Z is for <u>zap</u>.
Z is for zebras
reading a <u>map</u>.

Rhyme Chain

1. Reproduce the **Rhyme Chain Picture Cards reproducibles (pages 30–33)**. Show students the card with the word *hat*. Explain that they will be creating a rhyme chain for this word.

2. Challenge students to think of as many words that rhyme with *hat* as they can. *(cat, bat, rat, fat, mat, splat)* Refer to the Rhyming Word Families reproducibles (pages 8–10) for additional rhyming word ideas.

3. Write each rhyming word on a construction paper strip. Cut a slit through the dotted line on the hat card. Attach the first paper strip to the card by threading it through the slit. Use tape to connect the two ends of the strip together to create a link. Create another link using a blank construction paper strip. Continue alternating word strips with blank strips until you have added all the words to the card. The words on the alternating strips will all show forward so they can be easily read at a glance.

4. Attach the card and connected paper links to a bulletin board. On another day, choose a different word and picture card from the Rhyme Chain Picture Cards and repeat the activity. Display the rhyme chains around the room. Invite students to compare the lengths of the chains. Review the word chains all year and incorporate more difficult word families as the year progresses.

Rhyme Chain Picture Cards

hat

fish

bell

map

Rhyme Chain Picture Cards

bed

cake

bug

ball

Rhyme Chain Picture Cards

crow

dog

crown

sock

Rhyme Chain Picture Cards

sheep

ring

dice

sack

CHAPTER 2

Sound Search Street

The ability to hear and discriminate sounds is a necessary and basic skill in the development of phonemic awareness. The ability to hear and manipulate individual phonemes in words is critical to acquiring the English language code needed in order to read. The activities in this chapter give students the opportunity to identify sounds that are the same in isolation and within words.

Odd Man Out

1. Reproduce the **"Odd Man Out" Word List reproducibles (pages 35–36)**. The word list contains groups of sounds and words in which one is the "odd man out."

2. Explain to the class that Odd Ollie is always trying to fit in with the rest of the group, but he is always just a little bit different. When he tries to blend in and sound the same, the others always shout his name:

   Ollie, Ollie, you're too odd.
   They look around and then they nod.
   We say things that sound the same.
   We know that you are not to blame.
   But odd is odd so this we shout,
   Sorry, Ollie, you must get out!

3. Tell students that you will be saying several sounds or words. All of them will "fit in" except one. Ask students to find the "odd man out" and remove him from the group. When students identify the odd sound or word, invite them to say: *Sorry, Ollie, you must get out! _____ is the odd man out.* For example, if you say the three sounds /k/, /t/, /k/, students would reply: *Sorry, Ollie, you must get out!* **/t/** *is the odd man out.* Reinforce students' response by saying: *Great job!* **/t/** *is the odd man out because the other two sounds both say* **/k/**.

"Odd Man Out" Word List

Say aloud a group of words or sounds. Invite students to identify which one is the "odd man out." The sound or word in the group that does not belong is in **bold** type.

PHONEME DISCRIMINATION

/l/-/m/-/m/

/n/-**/m/**-/n/

/d/-/d/-**/p/**

/f/-/t/-/t/

/s/-/s/-**/z/**

/z/-/z/-**/b/**

/p/-**/k/**-/p/

/v/-**/l/**-/v/

/b/-/b/-**/d/**

/k/-/t/-/t/

/g/-**/j/**-/g/

/r/-/r/-**/w/**

WORD DISCRIMINATION

dirt-dirt-**cat**

at-car-car

bike-**run**-bike

two-two-**one**

cup-**mug**-cup

can-can-**slip**

doll-doll-**lion**

blue-**red**-blue

bug-**log**-bug

ship-**grow**-ship

truck-truck-**tip**

mine-pink-pink

BEGINNING SOUND DISCRIMINATION

cap-cold-can-**pat**

sit-**hat**-six-so

top-hit-hot-him

stand-stop-**gab**-stir

truck-trick-trim-**grip**

bat-bit-ball-**nut**

man-must-**tack**-mat

run-**dip**-red-rat

shin-thumb-think-thing

chick-chin-**slop**-chat

dog-dip-**bug**-dug

note-**sit**-night-net

ENDING SOUND DISCRIMINATION

stop-keep-jump-**rice**

pick-dot-seat-fit

find-ride-**flow**-sled

jog-mug-**did**-bug

hook-win-clown-mine

boil-**ten**-mile-wheel

room-him-game-**deal**

sick-cake-**skin**-pack

cash-fish-rush-**tall**

state-nest-**flake**-heat

wink-hear-car-score

mall-**grind**-whale-meal

"Odd Man Out" Word List

Say aloud a group of words. Invite students to identify which one is the "odd man out." The word in the group that does not belong is in **bold** type.

MEDIAL SOUND DISCRIMINATION

mut-**mat**-cut-rut

tell-pen-**had**-net

cape-late-sail-**pick**

king-cab-mad-jam

deep-**chill**-heel-meat

bug-duck-**chain**-hum

spin-kick-lid-**pine**

might-tile-fine-**cow**

bash-**dear**-tab-sack

bit-wish-**top**-skip

male-rain-late-**line**

came-pit-hip-hit

ENDING SOUND DISCRIMINATION

fall-**milk**-ball-wall

hook-shook-look-**stood**

clear-**weed**-fear-near

did-kid-**spring**-slid

snow-**globe**-throw-crow

spam-spring-wing-swing

tank-tug-plug-mug

bright-fight-**tried**-tight

when-then-pen-**step**

skunk-**bump**-chunk-bunk

kind-mind-blind-**bloom**

pump-poke-smoke-joke

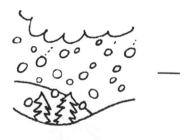 —   —

Tongue Ticklers

Using alliteration is a wonderful way to practice sound identification.
Print the following sentences on the board or on sentence strips. Say
the sentences one at a time, pointing to the first letter of each word as
you read. Invite students to tell you the sound that is the same in each
sentence. Repeat the activity as many times as you like or divide the
sentences over several days or weeks. Encourage students to recite these
fun tongue ticklers along with you. Then challenge students to create
their own!

Sample Sentences

Annie Ant asks about Aiden's apples.

Baby bees bring big bears berries.

Cute cuddly cats can catch colds.

Dizzy ducks dance during dinner.

Every elephant eats extra eggs.

Five flicking frogs follow fat flies.

Goofy goats gobble green grass.

Happy Holly hid handsome Harry's hat.

Icky insects inch into igloos.

Jolly Jamal juggles jelly jars.

King Karl kisses kind kittens.

Little lion licks lovable Larry's lunch.

Munching monkeys make many messes.

Naughty Nick needs new neighbors.

Oscar Octopus occupies odd Ollie.

Porky pink pigs pick purple pansies.

Quiet queens quickly quilt.

Rotten Raul rocks Rachel's rowboat.

Sappy Sandy sang sad songs.

Tricky Tran tickles turtles' tails.

Ugly uncles umpire under umbrellas.

Vickie's violet violin vanished.

Wacky Wendy will wish while we wait.

Ox fixes fox's six saxophones.

Yelping yaks yell, *Yippy-yi-yo!*

Zainy Zack zips Zoey's zipper.

Sound Off

Write the "Sound Off" chant on chart paper. Have students sit in a circle. Explain that military soldiers often chant a cadence as they march to help them stay in step. Teach students the chant and demonstrate how it will be a cue for them to brainstorm words that start with the same sound.

Sound Off

We know words that sound the same.
Let's see how many we can name.
Sit *and* ***stand*** *and* ***say*** *and* ***sack****,*
*All start with the letter **s***.
Sound off! ***S*** *words! Sound off!*

Repeat the chant, substituting different sounds and words.

Say What, Silly Sally?

1. Make a copy of the **Silly Sally Sound List reproducible (page 39)**. Tell students to turn on their listening ears because Silly Sally likes to say the same things. But sometimes Silly Sally gets mixed up and says different things too.

2. Tell students that if Silly Sally says the same thing, they should chant the word *same*. For example, tell students to listen to the beginning sounds in these words and say: *Silly Sally says* **man–map**. Students would chant the word *same* because both words start with the same beginning sound. If Silly Sally says *fat–can*, students would chant: *Say what, Silly Sally?* because the two words start with different beginning sounds.

3. Use the Silly Sally Sound List to help students recognize the same phonemes, beginning sounds, medial sounds, ending sounds, and rhyming words.

978-1-4129-5820-2

Silly Sally Sound List

Say a pair of sounds or words. Invite students to identify if they are the same or different.

PHONEMES

/j/-/j/	/b/-/k/	/d/-/b/	/p/-/p/
/f/-/g/	/l/-/l/	/h/-/m/	/z/-/v/
/n/-/n/	/qu/-/f/	/ch/-/ch/	/sh/-/s/
/th/-/v/	/r/-/r/	/x/-/z/	/y/-/w/

RHYMING WORDS

ban-bank	back-rack	pan-can	cup-rug
cap-lap	gash-hash	pay-pull	box-fox
wish-dish	miss-tag	fun-hug	sand-band
red-fed	soap-so	glide-ride	fix-trick

BEGINNING SOUNDS

mug-mad	rug-bug	Tim-dog	van-vase
tree-trick	wag-web	lip-pop	cat-car
grape-green	tip-rag	chair-trip	shell-shout
fall-tall	nail-nut	Sally-snail	think-thank

MEDIAL SOUNDS

pin-pit	can-cub	mop-flop	fun-sip
hen-red	lab-ran	zig-pug	win-kid
bun-fat	wig-rod	bat-cab	clock-dot
sheep-keep	cube-tub	shape-wake	cold-duck

ENDING SOUNDS

tan-fin	pet-box	find-read	lap-plan
car-fur	pack-lad	bunch-catch	clap-pup
fun-fuzz	mug-pig	tub-pick	wish-brush
with-wash	doll-bell	bus-books	word-man

Three Peas in a Pod

1. Reproduce the **Three Peas in a Pod** and **Pea Pod Picture Cards reproducibles (pages 41–45)**. Select and cut apart one set of picture cards (rhyming words, beginning sounds, medial sounds, or ending sounds).

2. Display the Three Peas in a Pod reproducible in the literacy center or use it with a small group. Mix up the picture cards you have selected. Invite a volunteer to find three picture cards that go together. For example, if you have chosen the rhyming words picture cards, a student might find the bat, rat, and cat cards. Ask the student to say the name of the pictures, tell why they go together, and place them in the circles inside the pea pod. Then, invite another student to find a matching set. Continue until all the cards have been matched.

3. For students with emerging skills, place the first picture card in the pea pod. Challenge a student to find the other two picture cards. For example, place the ball picture card inside the pea pod. Ask a student what sound the word *ball* begins with. Challenge the student to find two other picture cards that also start with the sound /b/. Use the same procedure for ending sounds or medial sounds.

Pea Pod Picture Cards: Rhyming Words

    bat-rat-cat

    bed-sled-bread

    bell-well-shell

    rain-chain-train

    man-pan-fan

Pea Pod Picture Cards: Medial Sounds

    /ŭ/: rug-bus-plug

    /ĭ/: hill-pig-stick

    /ŏ/: rock-fox-pot

    /ā/: whale-nail-rake

    /ē/: wheel-jeep-sheep

Pea Pod Picture Cards: Beginning Sounds

    /b/: ball-baby-banana

    /d/: dog-duck-door

    /h/: hand-heart-house

    /m/: mop-mitt-monkey

    /s/: scissors-sandwich-socks

Pea Pod Picture Cards: Ending Sounds

    /n/: sun-pin-hen

    /g/: bag-flag-leg

    /f/: leaf-giraffe-knife

    /r/: car-bear-deer

    /t/: carrot-net-hat

978-1-4129-5820-2

Three Peas in a Pod

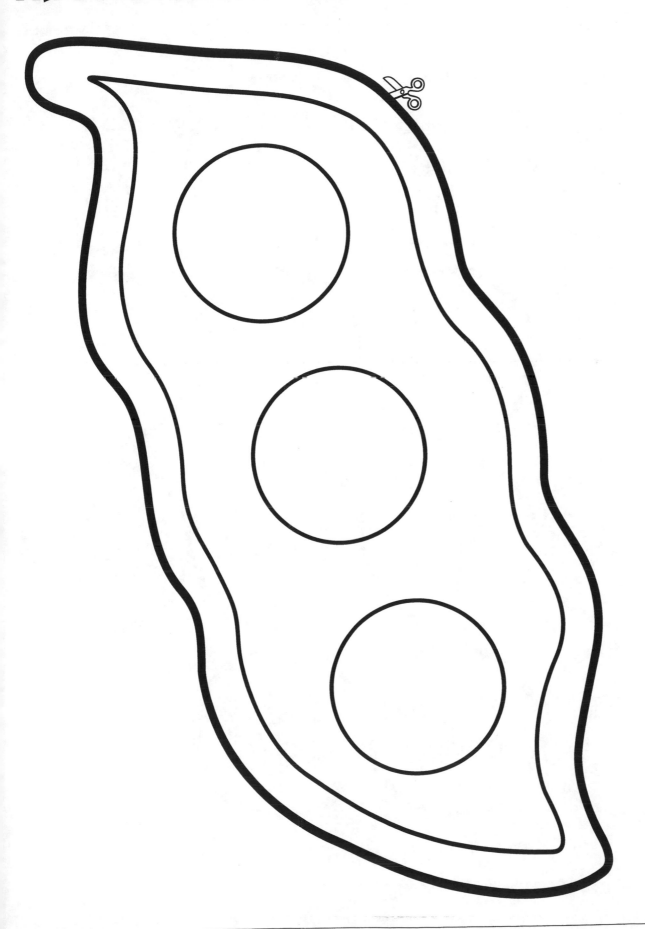

Pea Pod Picture Cards

RHYMING WORDS

I Ca Pod Picture Cards

BEGINNING SOUNDS

Pea Pod Picture Cards

MEDIAL SOUNDS

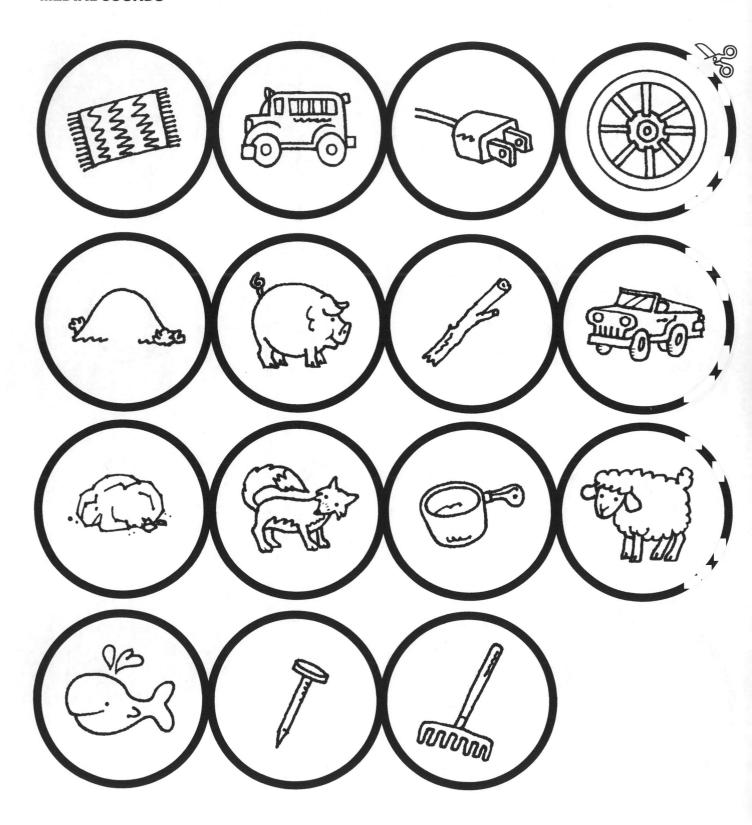

Pea Pod Picture Cards

ENDING SOUNDS

CHAPTER 3

Blending Boulevard

It is important for students to understand that words are made up of blended sounds. When we put two or more sounds together, we create a word. Begin oral blending exercises by asking students to blend larger word parts, such as syllables. Then, ask students to blend onsets and rimes. Finally, challenge students to blend whole words, sound by sound.

Retro Record Player

1. Explain to students that many years ago people didn't have CD players or MP3 players. They had a "retro" device called a *record player*. Tell students that the best thing about a record player was that you could speed up the record or slow it down. You could hear an entire song in slow speed.

2. Invite students to pretend they are listening to some retro records in slow speed as you say aloud some words and sounds. Tell them that when you give the cue, *speed it up*, they should say the word that you said very slowly at a normal speed. For example, say *cup . . . cake* very slowly in two parts. Then say: *Speed it up.* Students respond by saying: *Cupcake.*

3. Begin this activity by giving students syllables to blend. Then ask them to blend onsets and rimes and phonemes.

Syllables	Onsets and Rimes	Phonemes
touch-down	/f/-un	/k/-/ă/-/n/
six-teen	/f/-at	/p/-/ĭ/-/k/
can-dle	/k/-ick	/b/-/ŭ/-/z/
friend-ship	/ch/-ain	/v/-/ă/-/n/
can-dy	/m/-ask	/sh/-/ou/-/t/
snow-man	/r/-obe	/f/-/ĭ/-/l/
bed-room	/b/-all	/t/-/r/-/ŭ/-/k/
noo-dle	/m/-ad	/h/-/ă/-/n/-/d/

Trap It!

Tell students that they will be going on an imaginary nature walk. You will point out all of the wonderful creatures they will see. As you spot each creature, blend the creature's name slowly, so you don't scare it away. Then tell students to *trap it!* When you give this cue, ask students to cup their hands together and "trap" the word by saying it quickly. For example, say: *I spot a **/d/-/ē/-/r/**. Trap it!* Invite students to cup their hands together and say: *Deer!*

Forest Animals
bear	/b/-/ĕ/-/r/
deer	/d/-ē/-r/
bird	/b/-/ûr/-/d/
raccoon	/r/-/ă/-/k/-/o͞o/-/n/
bee	/b/-/ē/
squirrel	/s/-/kw/-/ûr/-/l/
beaver	/b/-/ē/-/v/-/ûr/

Farm Animals
horse	/h/-/ôr/-/s/
cow	/k/-/ou/
duck	/d/-/ŭ/-/k/
lamb	/l/-/ă/-/m/
sheep	/sh/-/ē/-/p/
chicken	/ch/-/ĭ/-/k/-/ə/-/n/
rabbit	/r/-/ă/-/b/-/ĭ/-/t/

Desert Animals
camel	/k/-/ă/-/m/-/ə/-/l/
snake	/s/-/n/-/ā/-/k/
rat	/r/-/ă/-/t/
lizard	/l/-/ĭ/-/z/-/ûr/-/d/
mouse	/m/-/ou/-/s/
spider	/s/-/p/-/ī/-/d/-/ûr/
hawk	/h/-/aw/-/k/

Ocean Creatures
shark	/sh/-/är/-/k/
fish	/f/-/ĭ/-/sh/
lobster	/l/-/ŏ/-/b/-/s/-/t/-/ûr/
eel	/ē/-/l/
starfish	/s/-/t/-/är/-/f/-/ĭ/-/sh/
whale	/w/-/ā/-/l/
dolphin	/d/-/ŏ/-/l/-/f/-/ĭ/-/n/

Scavenger Hunt

1. Choose an object that students can see in the classroom. Segment the word, sound by sound, very slowly using the following chant.

   Who can find it? Who can see,
   The /d/-/ĕ/-/s/-/k/ that's right in front of me?

2. Choose a student to blend the sounds together, say the word, and touch that object in the classroom. Invite that student to whisper the name of the next object in your ear.

3. Once students have become proficient at blending teacher-directed words, invite them to segment words for the class to blend. Try the same activity in other environments, such as the playground or library.

Swat It!

1. Draw a large grid on the board, or purchase an inexpensive picnic tablecloth and separate it into squares. In each square, write a different sound with which students are familiar.

2. Using a fly swatter, swat and say the sounds in a given word. For example, swat the v-a-n squares while saying the sounds slowly: */v/-/ă/-/n/*. Have students blend the sounds and chant the word together.

3. Repeat this activity using thematic words to go along with your classroom themes. This is also a great way to build vocabulary.

/g/	/b/	/v/	/f/	/a/
/m/	/d/	/z/	/t/	/ch/
/e/	/k/	/p/	/u/	/s/
/j/	/i/	/n/	/sh/	/o/

978-1-4129-5820-2

Who Done It?

Orally segment a series of story clues to help students guess "who done it." Segment each word sound by sound, by onset and rime, or by syllables. Challenge students to listen to each segmented word and blend the sounds together. Once students blend the first clue, write the blended word on the board. Repeat with the other story clues until students can guess the character or story that the clues describe.

Goldilocks and the Three Bears
Clue 1: /ch/-/âr/
Clue 2: /b/-/ĕ/-/d/
Clue 3: /b/-/ō/-/l/
Clue 4: /p/-/ôr/-/ĭ/-/j/

Itsy Bitsy Spider
Clue 1: /r/-/ā/-/n/
Clue 2: /s/-/p/-/ou/-/t/
Clue 3: /s/-/ŭ/-/n/
Clue 4: /s/-/p/-/ī/-/d/-/ûr/

Humpty Dumpty
Clue 1: /w/-/aw/-/l/
Clue 2: /f/-/aw/-/l/
Clue 3: /k/-/ing/
Clue 4: /h/-/ôr/-/s/-/ə/-/z/

Jack and Jill
Clue 1: /h/-/ĭ/-/l/
Clue 2: /f/-/ĕ/-/ch/
Clue 3: /w/-/aw/-/t/-/ûr/
Clue 4: /f/-/ĕ/-/l/

Three Little Pigs
Clue 1: /b/-/r/-/ĭ/-/k/-/s/
Clue 2: /s/-/t/-/ĭ/-/k/-/s/
Clue 3: /s/-/t/-/r/-/aw/
Clue 4: /h/-/ŭ/-/f/

Little Red Riding Hood
Clue 1: /g/-/r/-/ă/-/n/-/d/-/m/-/aw/
Clue 2: /b/-/ă/-/s/-/k/-/ə/-/t/
Clue 3: /w/-/o͝o/-/l/-/f/
Clue 4: /r/-/ĕ/-/d/

Stretchy Names

1. This activity is a great way for students to learn each other's names. Have students sit in a circle. Say the following chant using a student's name. Invite students to learn the chant and say it along with you.

   Benjamin, Benjamin, *how do you do?*
   Who's that friend right next to you?

2. Invite students to name the student sitting next to them when they hear their name in the chant. Ask students to say their neighbor's name in a very slow, stretched-out manner. Students can spread their hands to show how the name is stretched. For example, the class will chant: *Benjamin, Benjamin, how do you do? Who's that friend right next to you?* Benjamin will respond by saying his neighbor's name very slowly while spreading his hands: /m/-/ă/-/t/. The class will then use Matt's name in the chant to begin the process all over again.

3. Continue the activity until all students have had an opportunity to respond.

Story Time

Make copies of the **Story Time reproducibles (pages 51–54)**. Read aloud each story, one sentence at a time. Segment the sounds in the clue word in each sentence. Read the segmented words slowly so students can clearly hear each sound. Invite students to blend the segmented sounds together to make a word that answers each question.

Story Time

ON THE FARM

It was a /h/-/ŏ/-/t/ morning,
What kind of morning was it? (hot)

The farmer had to get up early to feed the /p/-/ĭ/-/g/-/z/.
What did he feed? (pigs)

When he got to the farm, he saw that the gate was /ō/-/p/-/ə/-/n/.
The gate was what? (open). The pigs were gone.

He didn't know where they went. Then the farmer heard a /l/-/ou/-/d/ crash.
What kind of crash did he hear? (loud)

He ran quickly back to his /h/-/ō/-/m/ to see what the noise was.
Where did he run? (home)

When the farmer opened the door, he started to /l/-/ă/-/f/.
What did he do? (laugh)

He saw the pigs sitting at the table eating /b/-/r/-/ĕ/-/k/-/f/-/ə/-/s/-/t/.
What were they eating? (breakfast)

AT THE ZOO

Going to the zoo is so much fun. The monkeys like to /s/-/w/-/ing/ from one side
of their cage to the other. *What do the monkeys like to do in their cage?* (swing)

If you listen really well, you can hear the lions and tigers /r/-/ôr/.
What do the lions and tigers do? (roar)

The elephants like to /s/-/t/-/ŏ/-/m/-/p/ around.
What do the elephants do? (stomp)

Everyone likes to feed the animals, especially the /d/-/ŭ/-/k/-/s/.
What does everyone like to feed? (ducks)

Kids can't wait to go back to the /z/-/o͞o/.
Where do the kids want to go? (zoo)

Story Time

A COLD DAY

One cold winter day my friend wanted to play in the /s/-/n/-/ō/.
Where did my friend want to play? (snow)

I put on my snow pants and /j/-/ă/-/k/-/ə/-/t/.
What did I put on? (jacket)

Finally, I put on my gloves and ran outside to make a /s/-/n/-/ō/-/b/-/aw/-/l/ to throw at my friend.
What did I make to throw at my friend? (snowball)

I waited, but he never came out. I knocked on the /d/-/ôr/ to see where he was.
What did I knock on? (door)

He fell asleep because he was so tired from trying to put on his snowsuit.
So, I made two more snowballs, and I turned them into a /s/-/n/-/ō/-/m/-/ă/-/n/.
What did I make? (snowman)

MOVIE MANIA

It is very exciting to go to the movie theater with a /f/-/r/-/ĕ/-/n/-/d/.
Who is it exciting to go to the theater with? (friend)

The popcorn is great to eat when it is has a lot of /b/-/ŭ/-/t/-/ûr/ on it.
Popcorn is good with a lot of what? (butter)

It is hard to choose only one box of /k/-/ă/-/n/-/d/-/ē/ because there are so many kinds.
What is hard to choose? (candy)

The best part is getting a big /s/-/ō/-/d/-/ə/ to drink.
What can we drink? (soda)

It is fun to listen to everyone laugh during the funny parts of the movie.
When you leave, don't forget to throw away all of your /t/-/r/-/ă/-/sh/.
What do you need to throw away? (trash)

Story Time

MANNERED ME

My mom says manners are the /k/-/ē/,
What are manners? (key)

Each day she must /r/-/ē/-/m/-/ī/-/n/-/d/ me.
What must she do? (remind)

Don't forget to say /p/-/l/-/ē/-/z/ and thank you too.
Don't forget to say what? (please)

For all I /h/-/ă/-/v/ and all I do.
For all you what? (have)

To cover my nose when I must /s/-/n/-/ē/-/z/,
When do you cover your nose? (sneeze)

And close my mouth when eating /p/-/ē/-/z/.
When eating what? (peas)

To open doors for filled up /h/-/ă/-/n/-/d/-/z/,
What is filled up? (hands)

I must do my part, do all I /k/-/ă/-/n/.
Do all you what? (can)

I should be thoughtful not to say /m/-/ē/-/n/ things,
What kind of things? (mean)

I should protect little /k/-/ĭ/-/d/-/z/ from bullying.
Protect who? (kids)

I tell my mom it's /p/-/l/-/ā/-/n/ to see,
What is it? (plain)

I'll be the best kid that I can be,
because she raised a mannered /m/-/ē/!
Who did my mom raise? (me)

Story Time

BIG PROBLEM

I've got a /l/-/ĭ/-/t/-/əl/ problem.
What kind of problem? (little)

Yes, it's really plain to /s/-/ē/,
It's plain to what? (see)

That my /k/-/r/-/ā/-/z/-/ē/ little brother really looks up to me.
What is my little brother? (crazy)

I know my /j/-/ŏ/-/b/ is difficult,
What is difficult? (job)

But yet it's /k/-/l/-/ē/-/r/ to me,
What is it to you? (clear)

That I must be the /b/-/ĕ/-/s/-/t/ big brother,
What must you be? (best)

I'll let him /l/-/ûr/-/n/ from me.
What can he do from you? (learn)

THE CIRCUS

At the circus there is so much to see and do.
The /c/-/l/-/ou/-/n/-/z/ like to make everyone laugh.
Who likes to make everyone laugh? (clowns)

They try to /j/-/ŭ/-/g/-/əl/ things.
What do they try to do? (juggle)

Clowns wear silly clothes, and their noses are /r/-/ĕ/-/d/.
What color are the clown's noses? (red)

You can also eat /p/-/ŏ/-/p/-/k/-/ôr/-/n/ at the circus.
What can you eat? (popcorn)

The circus is fun for kids and adults.
It will be exciting to go /ə/-/g/-/ĕ/-/n/.
When do you want to go? (again)

CHAPTER 4

Segmentation Sidewalk

Segmentation activities help students separate words into individual sounds. Hearing each phoneme within a word can be challenging for young students. Start with segmentation activities that focus on the number of words in a sentence. Then, progress to activities that break words into syllables. Finally, when students are proficient at counting syllables, challenge them to count individual phonemes in words.

Sentence Superheroes

1. Make copies of the **Sentence Strips reproducibles (pages 56–59)**. Cut apart the sentence strips and place them facedown in a pile on a table. Students will be counting the words in these sentences, but they do not need to be able to read the words. They will just need to recognize where one word ends and a new word begins by noticing the space between each unit.

2. Explain to students that they will become sentence superheroes. Their super power is being able to count the number of words in a sentence without even reading a single word.

3. Invite one student to choose a sentence strip from the pile, point to each word, and count the words aloud to the group. If the student correctly counts the number of words, respond by saying:

   You counted the words with all your might.
   You used your super powers right!

4. If the student incorrectly counts the number of words, correctly model how to count the words. Then say to that student:

   Your super powers will get it right.
   Please try again with all your might.

   Then invite the student to recount the words in the sentence.

5. Give each student an opportunity to count the words in a sentence.

Sentence Strips

I like to read.

She went out.

He is big.

He will help us.

Look at me.

The cookie was good.

The movie was funny.

Where are you?

I see you.

It is raining.

Sentence Strips

We will walk home.

I saw a green frog.

Sit down!

He bought some candy.

She sings a pretty song.

Sentence Strips

Tom ran away.

The brown bunny slept.

He cleaned his room.

It is sunny today.

These books are better.

Word Bites

1. Give each student two or three copies of the **Word Bites Chart reproducible (page 61)**. In this activity, students will count the number of words in a sentence that they hear orally.

2. Explain to students that Marvin Monster's mommy has always told him not to bite off more than he can chew. Marvin needs to take his time and take careful "word bites" when munching on his morning sentences. As Marvin bites his sentences, he needs to count each word and then color in one space for each word he hears. For example, in the sentence, *Marvin loves munching*, Marvin would color in three word bite squares because there are three words in the sentence.

3. Begin this activity by reading one of the two-word sentences provided below. Invite students to color in one square on their Word Bites Chart for each word they hear. Continue with the other sentences or create sentences of your own.

4. Challenge students to count words in three-, four-, and five-word sentences. Instead of coloring the squares, students can place a counter, such as a penny or small piece of candy, in each square to represent each word they hear.

Word Bite Sentences

Mary runs.

Babies cry.

Dogs bark.

Don is drawing.

Jan is happy.

They are racing.

Ann picked a flower.

The cat was purring.

The little boy laughed.

The tall man was reading.

The bell was ringing loudly.

Rob and Tom were playing.

978-1-4129-5820-2

Name _____ Date _____

Word Bites Chart

Directions: Count the number of words you hear in each sentence. Color in one square for each word you hear.

Silly Syllables

1. Explain to students that words can be broken into special parts called *syllables*. Teach students the following ways to check how many syllables are in a word.
   - "Check it with your chin" by holding your hand under your chin and counting how many times your chin hits your hand when you say a word.
   - Clap the word parts.
   - Tap the word parts on your arm.
   - Bounce a ball for each word part.

2. Invite students to try each of these techniques. Then tell them that today they are going to use the ball-bouncing technique to count the syllables in their names.

3. Have students sit in a circle. Begin the activity by saying a student's name. Slowly bounce a ball as you break the name into syllables. Invite students to count the syllables in the name by counting how many times you bounce the ball.

4. After modeling the activity, pass the ball to a student and say: *Silly, silly flea, tell us how many syllables your name should be.* Invite that student to respond by bouncing the ball as the class says the student's name in parts.

5. After the student bounces the ball and announces how many syllables are in his or her name, ask the class to clap the syllables to see if the answer is correct.

6. Continue the activity until all students have had the opportunity to count the syllables in their name. On another day, repeat the activity using students' last names.

978-1-4129-5820-2

Syllable Song

1. Write the following "Syllable Song" on chart paper. Have students gather on the rug to listen as you sing the song.

   ### Syllable Song

   (Tune: "Do Your Ears Hang Low?")

   Do you hear word parts?

   Can you hear where words should break?

   Can you count them on your chin,

   To see how many taps it takes?

   Can you stretch them with a rubber band

   Or clap them with your hands?

   Do you hear word parts?

2. Ask students if they heard any special ways to count syllables as they listened to the song. Review the syllable-counting methods. *(clap them, stretch them with a rubber band, or count them on your chin)*

3. Suggest a theme such as classroom objects or favorite characters. Invite students to select a word that fits the theme and demonstrate how to count the syllables in that word using a technique from the "Syllable Song." For example, if a student chooses the word *computer* from the classroom object theme, the student could clap his or her hands to count three syllables. *(com-pu-ter)* The student would then tell the class that *computer* has three syllables. Another student may choose the word *bookshelf* and stretch out the word using a rubber band. The student would tell the class that *bookshelf* has two syllables. *(book-shelf)*

4. Continue the activity until every student has a chance to count the syllables in a word. Repeat the activity using different themes.

Speeding Syllables

1. Reproduce the **One-Syllable, Two-Syllable, Three-Syllable,** and **Four-Syllable Picture Cards reproducibles (pages 65–68)**. Cut apart the picture cards and place them in a basket.

2. Tell students that when you drive a car you need to know where to stop. Stop signs tell drivers where to stop. The stop signs break up the road into parts. Words can also be broken into parts.

3. Give each student a copy of the **Speeding Syllables reproducible (page 69)** and several small pieces of candy. Tell students that the stop signs are going to help them count how many syllables or parts are in different words.

4. Reach into the basket and select a picture card. Tell students what the picture is and model how to count the syllables using the Speeding Syllables chart. For example, if the word is *pencil*, say *pen* and move the candy to the first stop sign. Say *cil* and move the candy to the second stop sign. Emphasize each syllable while moving the candy from one stop sign to the next. Explain to students that the word *pencil* has two syllables because the candy is on the stop sign with the number *2*.

5. Choose another word from the basket and invite students to try the activity with you. Have students say the word and then repeat it again slowly while moving their candy the same way you demonstrated. You might want to begin the activity using only one- and two-syllable words, and then progress to three- and four-syllable words.

978-1-4129-5820-2

One-Syllable Picture Cards

car

bear

snake

cheese

plant

fork

book

clock

mouse

ring

bus

barn

Two-Syllable Picture Cards

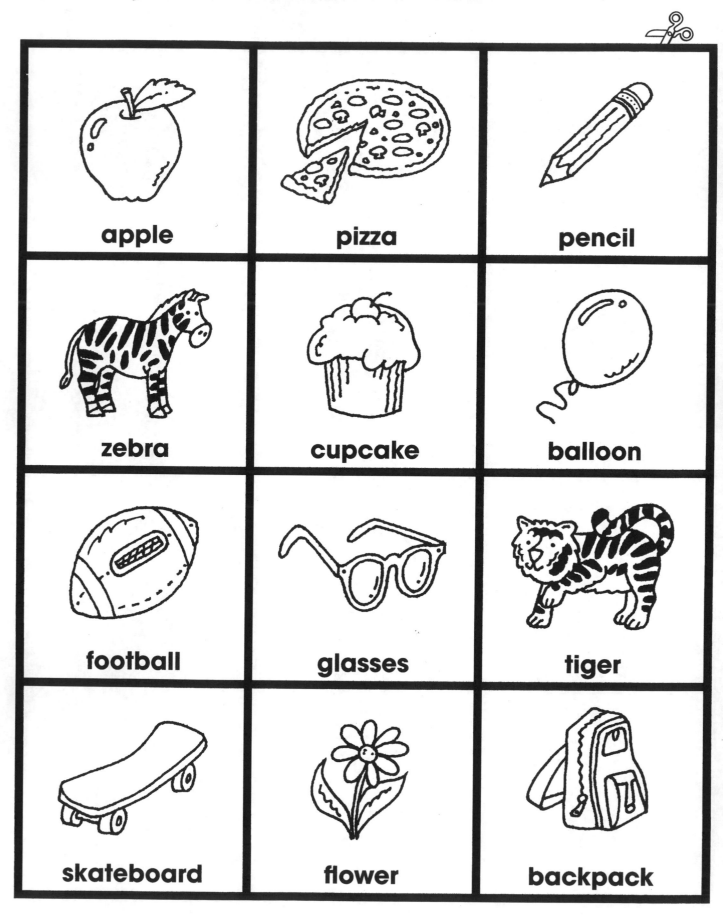

apple	pizza	pencil
zebra	cupcake	balloon
football	glasses	tiger
skateboard	flower	backpack

Three-Syllable Picture Cards

bicycle

tomato

computer

microscope

basketball

submarine

umbrella

elephant

octopus

strawberry

hamburger

cheerleader

Four-Syllable Picture Cards

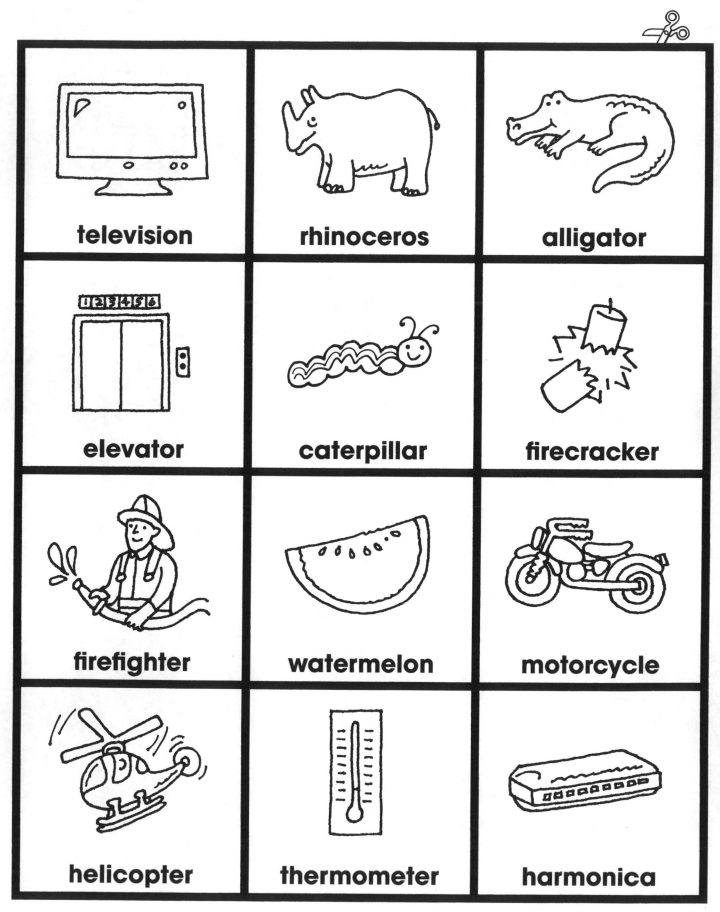

television

rhinoceros

alligator

elevator

caterpillar

firecracker

firefighter

watermelon

motorcycle

helicopter

thermometer

harmonica

Name _____ Date _____

Speeding Syllables

Directions: Use the stop signs to help you count syllables in words.

Start Here

Sassy Syllables

1. Reproduce the One-Syllable, Two-Syllable, Three-Syllable, and Four-Syllable Picture Cards reproducibles (pages 65–68). Cut apart the pictures and place them in a basket.

2. Give each student a pair of inexpensive gloves, such as white cotton gloves or latex gloves. Invite students to use art supplies to decorate their gloves if you wish. Then ask them to put on their "clapping gloves."

3. Choose a picture card from the basket and say the word. Invite students to clap the number of syllables as they repeat the word. Continue drawing picture cards from the basket and inviting students to clap out the syllables.

Syllable City

1. Divide students into small groups of two or three, or place the game in the literacy center. Create a set of laminated One-Syllable, Two-Syllable, Three-Syllable, and Four-Syllable Picture Cards (pages 65–68). Then enlarge and photocopy onto cardstock the **Syllable City Game Board reproducible (page 71)**. Provide various game pieces.

2. Tell students that in the Syllable City game they will be walking through town on their way to school. Have players stack their syllable picture cards facedown in one stack. Each player will choose a picture card, say the name of the picture, and tell how many syllables are in the word. If correct, the player moves one space for every syllable. For example, if a player draws the bus picture card and identifies that the word *bus* has one syllable, he or she would advance one space.

3. Invite students to take turns drawing cards and moving their game pieces around the board until one player reaches the school.

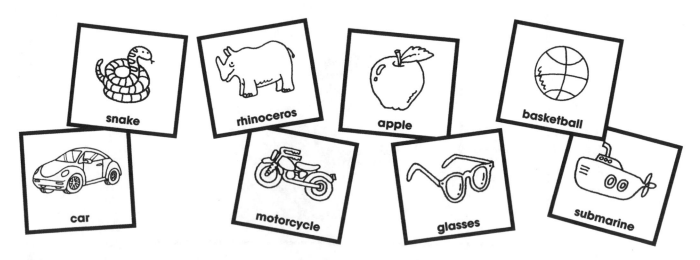

snake   rhinoceros   apple   basketball

car   motorcycle   glasses   submarine

Syllable City Game Board

				Ride the Bus Move ahead 1 space.		
Bus Stop Go back 2 spaces.						
			Accident Go back 2 spaces.			**65 MPH** Move ahead 2 spaces.

FINISH

| **Construction** Go back 1 space. | | | | | |

| | | | | **Stop Sign** Lose a turn. |

START

Demolition Derby

1. In this activity, students will segment words into onsets (initial consonant or consonant blend) and rimes (the vowel and all that follows). Explain to students that a demolition derby is a contest in which drivers crash old cars into each other until only one car is left running. This activity will be like a demolition derby, only instead of cars, students will be "crashing" words. They will break words apart into the beginning sound (that falls off just like a fender might fall off a car) and the leftover sound.

2. Make a copy of the Rhyming Word Families reproducibles (pages 8–10) to use as a word reference. Say a word for students and then shout: *CRASH!* Tell students this is their cue to say the first sound they heard and then the remaining part of the word. For example, if you say: *Land, CRASH!*, students should respond: */l/-/and/*.

Rubber Band Stretch

1. Reproduce the **Two-Phoneme**, **Three-Phoneme**, and **Four-Phoneme Picture Cards reproducibles (pages 77–79)**, cut apart the cards, and place them in a basket.

2. Select a card from the basket and model how to stretch a rubber band as you stretch out the sounds in the word. Then say the word quickly as you bring back the rubber band.

3. Give each student a rubber band. Continue selecting picture cards and invite students to practice the rubber band stretch as they slowly segment the sounds they hear in each word.

Lost and Found

1. In this activity, students will listen to two words and identify the sound that was omitted from the first word to make the second word. Ask students if they have ever lost something. Remind them that when they lose an item, such as a hat or a jacket, they can go to a lost and found department to try to find it. Tell students that they are going to listen to sounds in the "lost and found department."

2. Explain how to complete the activity. You will say two words and ask students to listen carefully to hear what sound was lost in the first word to make the second word. For example, say the two words *nice* and *ice*. When saying *nice*, emphasize the first sound by holding it longer than usual: *Nnnnn-ice*. Ask students to say the two words with you. Then ask them what sound was lost. Students should be able to identify that the /n/ sound was lost. Explain that when you take the /n/ sound away from *nice*, you get *ice*.

3. After students are able to identify a single lost consonant sound, challenge them to identify lost consonant blends and digraphs. Use the following word pairs or create your own.

Word Pairs

ball-all	fear-ear	dice-ice
wall-all	dear-ear	mice-ice
small-all	gear-ear	nice-ice
tall-all	hear-ear	rice-ice
	near-ear	slice-ice
band-and		
hand-and	fair-air	ditch-itch
land-and	chair-air	hitch-itch
sand-and	hair-air	pitch-itch
stand-and	stair-air	witch-itch
	pair-air	stitch-itch
boat-oat		
coat-oat	cape-ape	dart-art
goat-oat	tape-ape	chart-art
moat-oat	drape-ape	part-art
	scrape-ape	start-art
bold-old	grape-ape	smart-art
sold-old		
cold-old		
hold-old		
mold-old		

1, 2, 3, Count with Me

1. Reproduce the Two-Phoneme, Three-Phoneme, and Four-Phoneme Picture Cards reproducibles (pages 77–79), and cut apart the cards. Explain to students that they will be playing a counting game to see how many sounds they hear in a word.

2. Show students a picture card and tell them that you need help identifying it. Ask students what picture they see. Challenge one student to tell you how many sounds he or she hears in the word. For example, for the duck picture card, the student would identify three sounds in the word *duck* (/d/-/ŭ/-/k/). Keep in mind that students are counting sounds, not letters.

3. Give the card to the student who correctly identifies the phonemes. Continue the activity until all the cards are distributed to students.

Two-Phoneme Words	Three-Phoneme Words	Four-Phoneme Words
ax	sock	crab
egg	pig	lamp
bee	bat	camel
pie	bell	tent
key	duck	nest
hay	lock	bread
ice	mat	dress
ear	can	block
tie	box	frog
paw	top	brush
boy	cat	ladder
cow	rope	stars

978-1-4129-5820-2

Sound Match

1. Make copies of the **Sound Match reproducible (page 80)**. Cut apart the two game boards. Divide the class into small groups of three or four and give a game board and some counters to each student in the groups.

2. Reproduce a set of Two-Phoneme, Three-Phoneme, and Four-Phoneme Picture Cards reproducibles (pages 77–79) for each group of students. Cut apart the cards and place them in a pile.

3. Invite the first player in each group to choose a card from the top of the pile, say the picture name, and count the number of sounds in the word. Have the student use a counter to cover a number on the game board that corresponds with the number of sounds in the word. For example, if a student draws the lamp picture card, he or she would place a counter over the number 4 on the game board because the word *lamp* has four sounds. If a student draws a picture card for which there is no number left to cover, he or she loses a turn. The first student to cover every number on the game board wins.

Sound Check

1. Reproduce the Two-Phoneme, Three-Phoneme, and Four-Phoneme Picture Cards reproducibles (pages 77–79), cut them apart, and place them in a basket.

2. Give each student a write-on/wipe-off board and a marker. Select a picture card from the basket and call out the word. Invite students to count the sounds and write the number of sounds they heard on their write-on/wipe-off board.

3. Have students hold up their boards for a "sound check."

Sound Around

1. Reproduce the Two-Phoneme, Three-Phoneme, and Four-Phoneme Picture Cards reproducibles (pages 77–79), cut them apart, and place them in a basket.

2. Invite students to sit in a circle. Have the first student draw a card from the basket and say the name of the picture card. Ask him or her to tell how many sounds are in the word. Then have the student pass the basket to the next student.

3. Continue until each student has had a turn.

Two-Phoneme Picture Cards

Three-Phoneme Picture Cards

Four-Phoneme Picture Cards

Sound Match

2	4	3
4	3	2
3	2	4
2	2	3

Sound Match

4	2	4
3	2	3
2	4	4
3	4	2

Quick Draw

1. Divide the class into pairs. Reproduce the Two-Phoneme, Three-Phoneme, and Four-Phoneme Picture Cards reproducibles (pages 77–79). Cut apart the cards and give each pair of students a set of picture cards stacked in a facedown pile.

2. Have each player draw a card at the same time, say the name of the picture, and count the sounds. The student who draws the card with the most sounds keeps both cards. For example, if the first player draws the can picture card, which has three sounds (/k/-/ă/-/n/), and the second player draws the car picture card, which has two sounds (/k/-/är/), the first player would keep both pictures. If the two cards have the same number of sounds, have students draw again. After the second draw, the student who draws the card with the most sounds keeps both pairs of cards.

3. Have players continue until all of the cards are drawn. The student with the most cards wins.

Sound Sort

1. Reproduce the Two-Phoneme, Three-Phoneme, and Four-Phoneme Picture Cards reproducibles (pages 77–79), and cut apart the cards. Prepare a set of cards for each pair of students. Give each student or pair of students a copy of the **Sound Sort Chart reproducible (page 82)**.

2. Invite students to work independently or with a partner to sort the picture cards by the number of sounds they hear in each word. Have students pick up a card, say the picture name, count the sounds, and place the card in the correct column. For example, if a student picks up the bell picture card, he or she would place it in the "3 Sounds" column to show that the word *bell* has three sounds (/b/-/ĕ/-/l/).

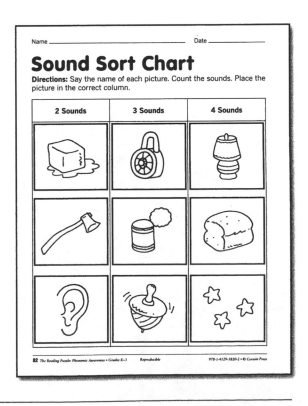

Name _____   Date _____

Sound Sort Chart

Directions: Say the name of each picture. Count the sounds. Place the picture in the correct column.

2 Sounds	3 Sounds	4 Sounds

"Sing a Song" Sound Count

Counting individual phonemes can be difficult for students. To help students with this skill in a fun and engaging way, teach them songs and chants. Make a transparency of **"Sing a Song" Songs reproducibles (pages 84–85)**, or write the lyrics on chart paper. Model for students how to sing the songs and explain what their part will be in the activity. Use the words from the list below for phoneme segmenting practice in the songs and chants. As students learn each song, challenge them to create new verses and segment new words.

Two Phonemes
at
it
show
now
two
say
up
pie
why
out

Three Phonemes
map
bat
phone
cap
pop
hip
ran
chip
sick
sight

Four Phonemes
bump
steal
flame
brain
smash
pest
treat
broke
puzzle
water

Five Phonemes
skunk
plump
plant
folder
bucket
scissors
rabbit
zebra
ticket
tennis

"Sing a Song" Songs

Clementine

(Tune: "Clementine")

Count the sounds, count the sounds,
Words have sounds that you can hear.
Count the sounds in this next word,
If you're right, we'll give a cheer.

Teacher: Goat!

Students: Three sounds!

Teacher: /g/-/oa/-/t/
(Hold up a finger for each sound.)

Happy Sounds

(Tune: "If You're Happy and You Know It")

Teacher: If you're happy and you know it, count the sounds.
If you're happy and you know it, count the sounds.
If you can hear all the sounds, then you can count them out.
If you can count the sounds, shout it out—**sun**!

Students: Three!

Teacher: /s/-/u/-/n/
(Hold up a finger for each sound.)

"Sing a Song" Songs

Shout Out

(Tune: "Sound Off" Military Cadence)

Teacher: Children, children, have you heard?
There are sounds in all the words.
These are sounds that you can count.
Try it now and shout it out!

Teacher: Star—Shout out!

Students: Three sounds!

Teacher: /s/-/t/-/ar/
(Hold up a finger for each sound.)

Clap Them Out

(Tune: "If You're Happy and You Know It")

If you can hear the sounds in **man**, clap them out.
If you can hear the sounds in **man**, clap them out.
If you can hear the sounds in **man**,
Then for each sound clap your hands.
If you hear the sounds in **man**, clap them out. **/m/-/a/-/n/**

If you can hear the sounds in ___, clap them out,
If you can hear the sounds in ___, clap them out.
If you can hear the sounds in ___,
Then for each sound clap your hands.
If you hear the sounds in ___, clap them out.

CHAPTER 5

Manipulation Mile

Magical Mumbles

This engaging activity will help students see that language can be creative and imaginative. You will be using nonsense sequences to teach students about alliteration.

1. Explain to students that in the story, *Cinderella*, the Fairy Godmother sings *bippity, boppity, boo* to make her magic happen. Invite students to repeat the phrase after you. Help them recognize that each word begins with the /b/ sound.

2. Invite them to replace the beginning /b/ sound with the /p/ sound to create the phrase *pippity, poppity, poo.*

3. Tell students that you will say a sound and they will use that sound at the beginning of each word in the magical phrase. Wear a crown and wave the magic wand as you direct students to create the following nonsense magical phrases.

/n/	nippity, noppity, noo
/d/	dippity, doppity, doo
/m/	mippity, moppity, moo
/t/	tippity, toppity, too
/st/	stippity, stoppity, stoo
/s/	sippity, soppity, soo
/h/	hippity, hoppity, hoo
/f/	fippity, foppity, foo
/r/	rippity, roppity, roo
/ch/	chippity, choppity, choo

Who's That?

1. Tell students that you are going to call them to the rug by name. Warn them that because you accidentally spilled something on your attendance book, the names are smudged and hard to read.

2. Tell students to listen carefully. If they hear a name that sounds similar to someone in their class, they should ask: *Who's that?* and then say the student's correct name. The student whose name is called will join you on the rug.

3. Continue to call students to the rug until the entire class has joined you. Try the same game another day, changing medial or ending sounds instead of the beginning sounds.

Beginning Sound Manipulation

Teacher: *Come over to the rug, Batthew.*

Students: *Who's that? (Matthew)*

Teacher: *Come over to the rug, Farah.*

Students: *Who's that? (Sarah)*

Teacher: *Come over to the rug, Zim.*

Students: *Who's that? (Kim)*

Ending Sound Manipulation

Teacher: *Come over to the rug, Marf.*

Students: *Who's that? (Mark)*

Teacher: *Come over to the rug, Sap.*

Students: *Who's that? (Sam)*

Teacher: *Come over to the rug, Jilliam.*

Students: *Who's that? (Jillian)*

Medial Sound Manipulation

Teacher: *Come over to the rug, Put.*

Students: *Who's that? (Pat)*

Teacher: *Come over to the rug, Ruse.*

Students: *Who's that? (Rose)*

Teacher: *Come over to the rug, Toler.*

Students: *Who's that? (Tyler)*

Detect It

Tell students that they are going to be rhyme detectives. They need to listen to clues to be able to detect a new word. Invite students to listen to your clues and make phoneme substitutions to create new words. Once students are successfully able to substitute beginning sounds, increase the difficulty of the activity by challenging them to substitute ending sounds.

Beginning Sound Riddles

What rhymes with *cot* and starts with /d/?   (dot)

What rhymes with *but* and starts with /k/?   (cut)

What rhymes with *bet* and starts with /n/?   (net)

What rhymes with *cup* and starts with /p/?   (pup)

What rhymes with *hog* and starts with /sm/?   (smog)

What rhymes with *bell* and starts with /s/?   (sell)

What rhymes with *hit* and starts with /k/?   (kit)

What rhymes with *sag* and starts with /r/?   (rag)

What rhymes with *call* and starts with /f/?   (fall)

What rhymes with *pick* and starts with /ch/?   (chick)

Ending Sound Riddles

What starts like *but* but ends with /z/?   (buzz)

What starts like *sell* but ends with /d/?   (said)

What starts like *trip* but ends with /m/?   (trim)

What starts like *fan* but ends with /t/?   (fat)

What starts like *stun* but ends with /f/?   (stuff)

What starts like *chin* but ends with /k/?   (chick)

What starts like *ten* but ends with /l/?   (tell)

What starts like *dot* but ends with /n/?   (Don)

What starts like *pack* but ends with /s/?   (pass)

What starts like *hug* but ends with /m/?   (hum)

Eye Spy

Explain to students how to play this special Eye Spy game. Tell them that you are going to spy something and then take away part of the word. They will need to respond by telling you the new word after your prompt. For example, say: *I spy a doghouse without the dog. What do I spy?* Students should reply: *House.*

Tell students that some of the new words may be nonsense words or make-believe words. Begin the activity by deleting a word part and then progress to the deletion of a syllable, initial phoneme, final phoneme, initial phoneme in a blend, final phoneme in a blend, and the second consonant in an initial blend.

Word Parts

I spy a *cupcake* without the *cup*.	*(cake)*
I spy a *basketball* without the *basket*.	*(ball)*
I spy a *goldfish* without the *fish*.	*(gold)*
I spy a *notebook* without the *note*.	*(book)*
I spy a *sunflower* without the *flower*.	*(sun)*
I spy a *flashlight* without the *flash*.	*(light)*
I spy a *snowball* without the *ball*.	*(snow)*
I spy a *newspaper* without the *news*.	*(paper)*

Syllables

I spy a *flower* without the *flow*.	*(er)*
I spy a *cucumber* without the *cu*.	*(cumber)*
I spy a *basket* without the *bas*.	*(ket)*
I spy a *kitten* without the *kit*.	*(ten)*
I spy a *curtain* without the *cur*.	*(tain)*
I spy a *picture* without the *pic*.	*(ture)*
I spy a *tomato* without the *to*.	*(mato)*
I spy a *circle* without the *cir*.	*(cle)*

Initial Phonemes

I spy a *chair* without the /ch/.	*(air)*
I spy a *fence* without the /f/.	*(ence)*
I spy a *bicycle* without the /b/.	*(icycle)*
I spy a *meatball* without the /m/.	*(eatball)*
I spy a *nose* without the /n/.	*(ose)*
I spy a *book* without the /b/.	*(ook)*
I spy a *sandwich* without the /s/.	*(andwich)*

Final Phonemes

I spy a *trunk* without the /k/.   (trun)

I spy a *leaf* without the /f/.   (lea)

I spy a *chest* without the /t/.   (ches)

I spy a *pencil* without the /l/.   (penc)

I spy a *dress* without the /s/.   (dre)

I spy a *light* without the /t/.   (ligh)

I spy a *table* without the /l/.   (tab)

Initial Phoneme in a Blend

I spy a *snail* without the /s/.   (nail)

I spy a *glove* without the /g/.   (love)

I spy a *block* without the /b/.   (lock)

I spy a *flower* without the /f/.   (lower)

I spy a *truck* without the /t/.   (ruck)

I spy a *stove* without the /s/.   (tove)

I spy a *brick* without the /b/.   (rick)

Final Phoneme in a Blend

I spy a *friend* without the /d/.   (frien)

I spy a *nest* without the /t/.   (nes)

I spy a *band* without the /d/.   (ban)

I spy a *wasp* without the /p/.   (was)

I spy a *mask* without the /k/.   (mas)

I spy a *belt* without the /t/.   (bel)

I spy a *husk* without the /k/.   (hus)

Second Consonant in an Initial Blend

I spy a *blanket* without the /l/.   (banket)

I spy a *glass* without the /l/.   (gass)

I spy a *cliff* without the /l/.   (ciff)

I spy a *crash* without the /r/.   (cash)

I spy a *dragon* without the /r/.   (dagon)

I spy a *flame* without the /l/.   (fame)

I spy a *bridge* without the /r/.   (bidge)

I spy a *group* without the /r/.   (goup)

I spy a *plant* without the /l/.   (pant)

I spy a *present* without the /r/.   (pesent)

Mystery Stew

1. Make a copy of the **Mystery Stew Ingredients Cards reproducibles (pages 92–93)**. Color, laminate, and cut out the picture cards.

2. Put on a chef's apron and gather a cooking pot, spoon, and the Mystery Stew Ingredients Cards, and place them on a table. Tell students that you are going to be cooking a pot of mystery stew. Explain that you need to add all of the ingredients to the stew pot, but you will need their help. For this recipe all of the ingredients must begin with the /s/ sound.

3. Show students the first Mystery Stew Ingredients Card and say its name. Challenge students to change the beginning sound to /s/. Then drop the card into the cooking pot as students say the new ingredient's name. For example, show students the beef picture card. Tell them that you can't add beef to the stew because it does not begin with the /s/ sound. However, you can add _____. Invite students to fill in the blank by substituting the /b/ sound in *beef* to /s/ to make the nonsense word *seef*. Remind students that for this stew they will be creating mystery, nonsense ingredients.

4. Repeat the activity using other initial consonant sounds or by challenging students to manipulate the ending sounds of the ingredients.

Mystery Stew Ingredients Cards

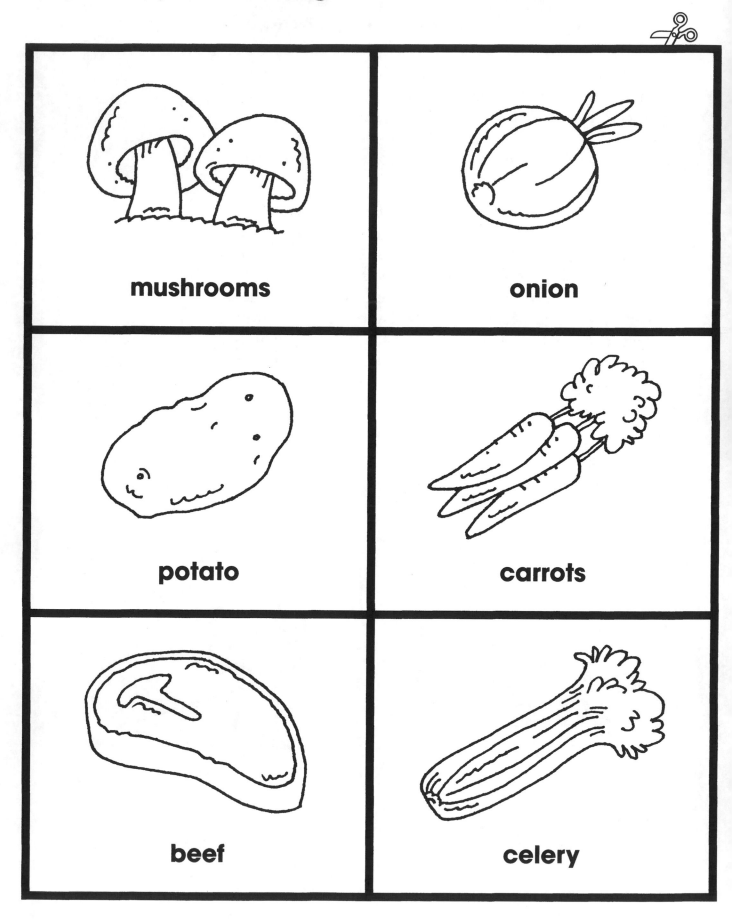

mushrooms

onion

potato

carrots

beef

celery

978-1-4129-5820-2 • © Corwin Press

Mystery Stew Ingredients Cards

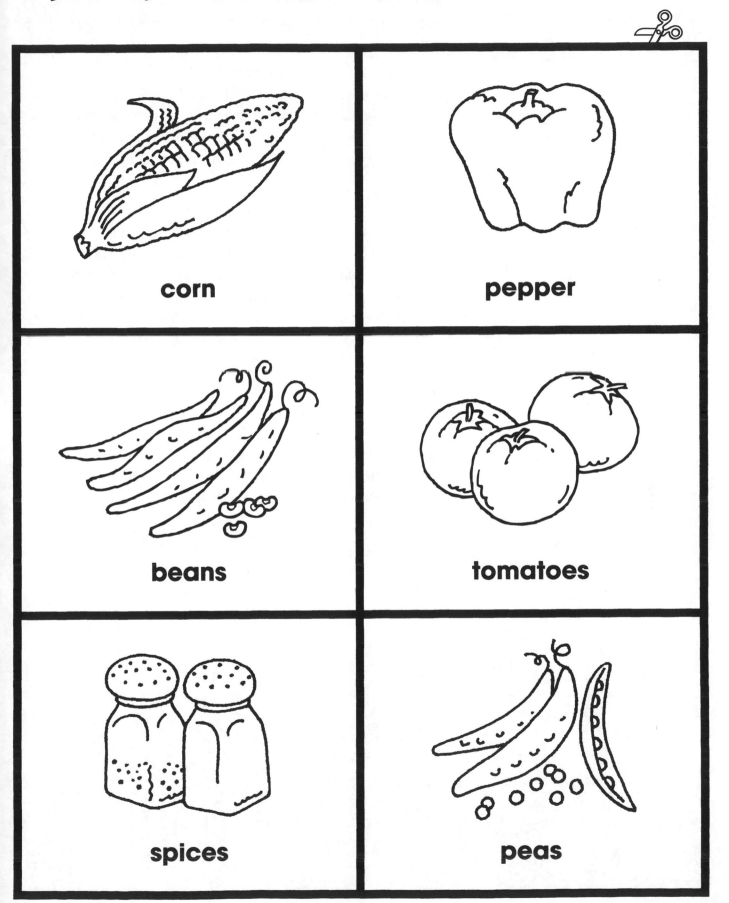

corn

pepper

beans

tomatoes

spices

peas

Choo, Choo, Choose the Sound

1. Give each student a copy of the **Sound Train Cars reproducible (page 95)**. Invite students to color the train cars and cut them out.

2. Have students place the three train cars in front of them in order (engine, passenger car, and caboose). The three train cars represent three types of sounds in words. The engine represents the beginning sound of a word. The passenger car represents the medial sound of a word. The caboose represents the ending sound of a word.

3. Tell students that you are going to say two words that are the same except for one sound. Challenge students to use their train cars to show which sound has changed in the word. For example, if the two words are *sick* and *kick*, students should choose the train engine, slide it up, and say: *Choo.* This will show that the sound that changed was the first sound in the word. If the words are *lock* and *lick*, students should slide up the passenger car and say: *Choo, choo.* This will indicate the changed sound was in the middle of the word. If the ending sound is changed, students should slide up their caboose and say: *Choo, choo, choo,* to indicate the ending sound was changed.

Engine Words (Beginning Sound Change)	Passenger Car Words (Medial Sound Change)	Caboose Words (Ending Sound Change)
mill-fill	mug-meg	cute-cube
rod-pod	rat-rot	name-nail
me-see	hug-hag	kid-kit
dry-try	net-nut	coat-coal
said-red	sit-sat	bat-bad
pot-cot	pit-pat	like-life

978-1-4129-5820-2

Sound Train Cars

Directions: Color and cut out each train car. Use the train cars to show where you hear the changed sound in each word. ✂

References

Fry, E. B., Kress, J. E., & Fountoukidis, D. L. (1993). *The reading teacher's book of lists*. Paramus, NJ: Prentice Hall.

Hall, S. (2006). *I've dibel'd, now what?* Longmont, CO: Sopris West Educational Services.

McEwan, E. K. (2002). *Teach them all to read: Catching the kids who fall through the cracks*. Thousand Oaks, CA: Corwin Press.

Young, S. (1994). *Scholastic rhyming dictionary*. New York, NY: Scholastic.

Printed in the United States
By Bookmasters